What the Rivers Gather

Selected Poems

Milton Jordan

STEPHEN F. AUSTIN STATE UNIVERSITY PRESS

Copyright © 2020 Stephen F. Austin State University Press
Printed in the U.S.A.

All rights reserved. No part of this book may be used or reproduced in any manner whatsoever without writen permission except in the case of brief quotations in critical ariticles or reviews.

For more information:
Stephen F. Austin State University Press
P.O. Box 13007 SFA Station
Nacogdoches, Texas 75962
sfapress@sfasu.edu
sfasu.edu/sfapress

Distributed by Texas A&M Consortium
tamupress.com

ISBN: 978-1-62288-313-4
First Edition

Many of these poems, or earlier versions of them, appeared in *Abraxas, Alternatives, The Bluegrass Literary Review, Boise Broadside, Buckle, Idaho Heritage, The Intermountain Observer, Plainsong, Scarab, Snapdragon, Spitball, The Texas Observer, Wind,* and in the anthology, *Poetry is Living in the Firelands* and the chapbook, *Better Things To Do* published by Bottom Dog Press.

*Life tires us
unless we can be
rejuvenated daily
by simplicities.*

- Elory Bode

CONTENTS

Some Idaho Poems

Salmon River Road	13
U. S. 95	14
On Slate Creek	15
B C Roadside	16
Listening	17
Midnight McCook, Nebraska	18
Firmer Footing	19
Since You Left	20
Another Journey	21
My Idea	22
Princess of Summer Squash	23
Faculty Parking Only	24
Final Examination	25
Lodgepole Pine	26
Turn It Over	27
Clean Toothed Saws	28
For A Sharper Blade	29
After Drilling Barren Wells	30
Ballad for Agrarian Reformers	31
Messages From A Littered Landscape	32
Cole's Dream	33
Spring Training	34
Early Spring, Late Light	35
Along a Steep Path	36
Urban Renewal	37
Hanging the New Exhibit	38

In the Firelands Ohio

Around A Bald Cypress Tree	41
Bobby Bonds Remembering	42
Warming Up	43
Early in the Season	44
You Learned Photography In Summer Term	45
After Halloween We Let the Sun Go Down Early	46
After Spring Break	47
Somewhere It Might Be Spring	48
Ritual Occasions	49
In The Purchase Of Real Estate	50
Blind Man's Bluff	51
Nighttown Street Corner	52
Thank You Note For A First Edition	53
Now and Then	54
At Woodwinds and Reeds	55
In Some Heat and Hurry	56
Off the Lakeshore	57
In The Office Numbered Con 4	58
Near Playhouse Square	59
On The Edge Of Town	60
Office Hours	61
In This Barnyard	62
An Explanation	63
Out of the Vapors of Rent and Habit	64
The Pretend Highwayman	65
An Eighth Grade Day	67
Junior English Substitute	68
Answering For A Mediocre Career	69

Better Things To Do

Day Labor	73
Inclusive Value	74
April First	75
And The Weekly Conversation	76
Harvest	77
Once A Dairy Farmer	78
Con Progression	79
Organizer	80
Unemployed	81
Working	82
Singing The Expectation Blues	83
Better Things To Do	84
Heading Home	85
Retreat	86
Putting It Together	87

Other Work

What the River Gathers	91
Watching To Hear	92
Paying Attention	93
Broken Obelisk	94
Boom Times	95
Questionable Accuracy	96
In Answer to Your Letter with the International Reply Coupon Enclosed	97
Unexplained Pilgrimage	98
Tales Too Tall	99
An Amberman Afternoon	100
Minimum Wage	101
Red Dirt Summer	102
Red Dirt Summer II	103

Waiting for Breakfast	104
Tracking The Time	105
Lyrics Never A Song	106
Imagining One More Conversation	107
In The Stuffed Envelope	108
Men of the Church	109
The Night Rider	110
South Broadway Bus	111
That Was Years Ago	112
A Small Orchestra	113
Going To and Fro Upon the Earth	114
Autumn Walk	115
The Great Blue Heron	116
What We Left Behind	117
A Half-Sonnet for Anne	118
Losing My Way	119
An Afterword	120

Some Idaho Poems

Salmon River Road

The river then was this valley's
only contractor. Not long ago
she bore her own heavy equipment
cut and levelled the only roadways
washed in springtime, the boulders away
and put last year's road to a new bed.
That left behind road an intruder
now crumbling over the river's edge

Crews explode the hillside to clear a stretch
of terrace and leave the new old road behind
bewildered, unwelcome in the valley
and unwanted by the travelers.
Awkward yellow cavalry rumble
back and forth in full parade dress
and sharp upright banners stand
stark indicators of the outcome.

Nearer the river's edge the new old road
will gain the mystery of little use
and seeming age will shade its presence.
Asphalt curves will dissolve, buckled
over cheat grass in the ice heaves
the road an historical attraction
as new seasons of nostalgians wonder
at old routes and destinations.

Trapped between lust for wheeling friction
and vague desire to find a welcome place
among the river's legitimate children,
the road awaits each spinning set of wheels
and catalogues memories of passing tires
hoping, perhaps, they are not the last.
The road feels the end as the beginning
and knows the river's reality.

U. S. 95

We had left later than planned
and Saturday drug itself out of
sluggish gray beginnings near Horseshoe Bend.
The radio sound of Linda Ronstadt
rattled from Dave's Pontiac dashboard
and we fell into miles of silence.
Near Riggins he suggested lunch
at a place we had been before
and I was driving when we left.

Right there, Dave said, just below the shoulder
of that ridge, the Salmon turns north.
I know that but no one cares.
Few care, he said, where a river goes
or if it goes anywhere.

Still the river rushed foaming over rocks
and slowly under twin bridges toward
its junction with White Bird Creek
where we climbed up toward Camas Prairie.

We could bypass the town, but Dave refused
and launched his annual Chief Joseph
history lesson along the switchbacks.
We climbed onto the high prairie
and rain clouds stormed into Grangeville,
settled into the lower saddles,
and Saturday gave up as it began.

On Slate Creek

Stones and boulders scattered over headland
and the mountain casts its first shadow.
Yesterday blew by chalky white
dusting every expectation
of campers wanting less grit in their eggs.

Well below flood stage the creek settles
for a gravel coated right of way
and the road curves past unthreatened.
Locust trees cling to the hillside
below the ridge protecting the house
abandoned years before.

I wonder who lived here she says,
though she is not asking me,
and left a Massey Ferguson tractor
with two Ford pickups to rust away there.
Did they plan a town and build this road
expecting settlers like themselves?
Though she is still not asking me.

B C Roadside

West of Trail the local junk hauler
dropped me when he turned off the highway.
Big semis roared past and sparse local
traffic ignored the boulder where I sat.

All of you who knew me paid close
attention, acting out your roles
before bare hillsides, a theater
workshop of humor and regret.

Six kids in a psychedelic van
yelled me aboard atop duffel bags
against the rear door, and barely slowed
their chattering conversations
until I left them in Osoyoos.

Listening

You have never been able to enjoy
silence she said and I nodded
silently but clearly frowning.
You fill all these empty spaces
with thoughts I would leave unspoken.
You need not remind me that unspoken
they would never have become thoughts.
I nodded again silently
and now I was smiling.

Midnight McCook, Nebraska

Our late train braking at the station
my body anticipated the stop
as our coach slowed and rocked back
against the coupling, waiting
several seconds for your absent voice,
or some final relaxation.

Firmer Footing

With a certain staggering on our way,
since walking has been harder in the rain
we are alone along this wall of brick.
Others left for home and warmth
and wonder, from their bus windows,
at our presence leaning against
this lately populated bare wall.

With a moving sense of opened ways
the smell and buzz of traffic action
steals our attention and cars and buses
do not waver or stop to ask why.
We have not asked, Is this the line back?
but huddle for protection against
the building and, on occasion, each other.

Since You Left

The committee narrowed the list to five
and I hear you're still in contention.
Your reviews are all quite good but for
Spinner at the college, of course.
The city has grown along the river
south up on second ridge where Obermeyer's
dairy once spread beyond view.

I still see the town straddle the river
and now the college where you enrolled
has buildings taller than all the trees.
You may know the professor who
replaced Spinner and is also contending.
She lives on second ridge but her kids
all go to school with Andy.

Another Journey

Goodbye. Tomorrow I will sit here
and you will be in some treeless place.
No, you went to Wyoming last August,
tomorrow you are leaving for Bastrop
State Park with those lost Pine trees.
Goodbye, anyway and please don't write.
Deliver my greeting to Sharon and Ben.
I will sit here, fingers interlaced
And remember them both.

My Idea

I had been standing, through the season, naked on a starched plain
on a starched plain alongside my platform.
The wind split before me past a linoleum pole.
Still, occasionally, I turned my head to catch in my
open mouth the whistling the wind carries—only the sound
only the sound.
In the time, in that time, I built an estate
of bells and strange water whirling, centered green
and shrank from the sight of whales and enormous eels
eels of great size
Still, occasionally, I turned my head to catch in my
open mouth the whistling the wind carries—only the sound
only the sound.
Now, and now, I have photographed the starched plain
and captured, captured in brittle film, the ringing wet estate.
For the clatter of emptiness withdrew before her
And our remuda she established anew along a shifting in front.
Now, and now, I lower my head to catch in my
open mouth the whistling her legs carry—only the sound.

Princess of Summer Squash

Mother named her Elizabeth MacLean Parker after her English aunt and Scots grandfather and wished her a renowned beauty or an accomplished classical musician.

Mother must have known her three older
brothers would call her Betty Mac and her
not quite red hair and nearly ruddy
appearance make her short of beauty
and way too rowdy for classical.

In reds and blues Betty Mac nicked
her name on a brown two inch leather belt
and bounced around the house singing
R A G G, M O P P, rag mop,
a song we taught her early.

In high school boys laughed and loved
every minutes of it. Betty Mac
made her name singing folk music,
old songs from Jimmy Rodgers
and Bill Monroe's Bluegrass Boys.

And at that summer's festival,
celebrating our county's one
previous famed export, the judges
crowned her Princess and Mother
cheered as loudly as any of us.

Faculty Parking Only

Pauline bought a red Dodge shortbed pickup
last August and washes her prize each week
with the care of a first time mother,
scrubs the tires with soap filled steel wool
and shines fenders with fresh chamois.
Monday through Friday at 3:45
she walks around it in the teachers' lot
east of Capital High School and students
shout, 'Give us a ride, Ms. Sundberg.'
hoping for a spot in the back.
After months her eyes still glisten
as bright as the gloss on those fenders.

Final Examination

The five questions in our final examination today reflect information we have not covered during the semester. Here are the questions:

1.) How many butterflies must light on your right hand before it is too heavy to lift?
2.) Would color make any difference?
3.) When the butterflies fly away, will the noise of their beating wings attract widespread attention?
4.) Would the butterflies fly out the window or leave through the door?
5.) Bonus: On the playing field, will butterflies remain in formation?

Here are the wrong answers. Any other answers are correct.
1.) Eleven.
2.) Orange Monarchs are not so heavy as the lavender.
3.) A sound like bare feet marching.
4.) Through the Triumphal Arch.
5.) Goals scored at the south end count double.
Each correct answer is worth 25 points. Your papers are due next Friday or at your own convenience.

Lodgepole Pine

The argument turned on a peculiar conceit
Lodgepole pine, Sunday's paper said,
served a thousand uses, ridge beams
pack frames and teepee skeletons.
I got no use for it, said the sawyer,
warps all to hell and springs out of the saw.
You can't even hold it.
I read it really grows fast, I said.
Just as soon leave it grow.
I read the Shoshone used it for everything.
They didn't cut it for two by fours, he said.

Turn It Over

To turn it over, boys, to turn it over,
to pull our necks from beneath the boot
and to fly, to fly from the tables
accountants keep, their ledgers, boys,
and receivables. Slam their terminal
screens against polished hardwood floors.

Shall we stand, people, face to face
with the intolerable registers
of repression and not shout the cry?
Work for our hands, freedom for our minds
justice for the brothers and the sisters.

Cry for timbermen and pattern cutters,
for sawyers and sewing crews.
Turn it over, boys, for Martinez,
for Charlene and for confidence,
for us all, boys, for us all.

Clean Toothed Saws

Strapped about with the tackle of industry
sawyers turned back from thigh deep snow
to the mill empty of timber, the walls
hung with frames and oil glistened blades.
Spring not yet cracked free of winter,
they sat and thumb whined their polished saws
argued with idle mill hands, rip saw crews
and two lumber graders, of winters
some famous winter gone long years before.
Talk tracked to board feet per acre
and bonuses years before and soon.

For A Sharper Blade

Each morning your indrawn breath expects
the scent of fresh cut pine or false fir,
and you loosen and tighten your grip
in duct tape repaired White Mules.
Each noon you forget yesterday's lunch
and remember mills where you have worked
and rip saws that had a better blade.
You inspect the cuts in two by fours
and squint to notice tiny flaws
well used blades have left behind.
Once, you remember the earlier days,
you fashioned a bat for Sammy
he used for over half a season.

After Drilling Barren Wells

In the hot evening of a hotter day,
tools stored but the dust will not settle,
our crowd grows smaller on the veranda.
Beer sits flat at the bottoms of glasses
on tables under two bare trees
strung with dimly glowing bulbs

The whores have lost interest in the night
sitting sullen in the doorways
of their adobe rooms with thin smiles
for men passing their stripes of light.

The sound of billiards played without talent
follows Celinda out of the bar
with two more pitchers and menus
from which we seldom order.
She turns up her jukebox volume over
the radios in those adobe rooms

Ballad for Agrarian Reformers

1, Sawmill Blues
This room, a vaulted roof coliseum,
whirs and clatters with whangs of metal
past our OSHA required ear muffs.
Saws flush dust to hang in dry air,
Goggles wrap around our heads
but we pulled surgical masks below
our chins to take pine dust filled breaths.
We ripped two hundred board feet, select,
out of seven rough trimmed logs.

2, Dreaming
That we found gardens, here, grown over
and narrow trails through scattered trees
to reach deep woods of pine, white and loblolly.
That we stood in green air to blow and drive
against all industry, against the fabric
and the tone of it without recoil.
That we did not feel its silent refusal
the sullen pull of it and its tow,
in the face of such zephyrs, such small winds.

3, Sure of Ourselves
But thick, never lacerating
squat emplacements on a landscape
scheduled for reforestation.
Less than echoes of the forest's silence,
its deep green cry along black river stones,
we stumble on industry's abrupt edge
and fall far short of all dreaming
we zephyrs here on the skirts of violence.

Messages From A Littered Landscape

Speak up, you old and silent homestead.
Tell me the habits of sharecroppers
and their children with broken washboards,
metal snaps grown dull in this summer sun.
I found broken plumbing stored in their barn,
neatly filed receipts for seed potatoes,
and ledgers of a year's transactions.

I will sit on the stoop, the porch collapsing
behind me, and question your relics,
rusted hinges, scraps of ragged cloth,
broken ceramics, some rotted beams
and one small drinking cup, still whole.

Cole's Dream

I wake up mornings weary, muscles stiff
and skin screaming for me to scratch.
I stretch and scratch, Belle, and all my dreams
 have turned to running, rocky land rising
and my horses always lame, Belle.
A hard climb and posses close behind,
in relays on always faster horses
and their weapons never empty.
The dreaming wearies me, Belle.
I do not sleep and in my dreams
I am running, never Younger.

Spring Training

Fingers curling out of crevices
like knuckles from a fist rags of old snow
hang toward the valley from a ridge above town.
Across the valley the booster club dozed one
of the bare hills that roll away north and east
to build a utility pole and chicken wire backstop
where twelve boys slide wrist straps
of fielders gloves over their handlebars
and coast back down into town.
Sarah watches the riders in and out
of view along the switchbacks.
Supper grows cold as dusk and a baseball
in tall grass beyond left center field.

Early Spring, Late Light

Sunlight filters under day long cloud cover
and reflects off our still bare trees.
Above a shadow line of roof peaks
and church steeples sunset shines yellow
on the brown grass hillside and flashing
panes in new apartment windows.
Rising horizons replace the clouds
and this brief passing light darkens.

Along a Steep Path

Beyond the theater across public
baseball fields a street becomes dirt road
and starts to climb toward old cottonwoods
where the settlers first came to live.
A mile beyond the end of asphalt
the dirt road gives way to the trail
more easily followed than seen.

At the creek's edge cottonwoods
force the trail up over the ridge.
Part gives way and winds down to find
a coulee in its meadow of secrets,
but the trail struggles beyond the ridge
toward the crest from which the creek
has long been descending.

Urban Renewal

Downtown, in our east end of downtown
carpenters and stone and mortar men follow
wrecking crews from building to building
a plodding development of new old fronts.
The old new fronts replaced to expose
brick and post Victorian masonry
and the bench between the Pastime Club
and the Salvation Army removed.

Casual laborers stalk back at midday
from the employment office unemployed.
A man and his old lady just off the highway
from Denver spread cardboard across the ground
between the last two trees on Grove Street.
The casual window washer shares his lunch
harvested at Colonel Sanders alley entrance.

Hanging the New Exhibit

In the middle of the second room
past the door of the gallery,
in the middle of that large room
surrounded by weavings from local
(not necessarily native) artists
under the obviously mounted
lighting fixture, a geometric design
nearly six feet tall, about two feet through
in one direction, four in the other,
structured of various sized double sided
planes, mirrors facing and turning
away from one another
scattered the glare and color of rugs,
ponchos and hangings in shades of rust,
gold, orange or brown, all the likely
colors of weavings by local
(not necessarily native) artists
illuminated by the obviously
mounted lighting fixture.

In the Firelands Ohio

Around A Bald Cypress Tree

Mildred and Andy grew up and still live in a small town. Ottawa marks the edge of a coastal plain seventeen miles south of the lakeshore. Every night Mildred and Andy walk across the town square around a Bald Cypress tree in the southwest corner and back home. About once a week they stop by the bookstore after it is closed and peer through the windows.

Mildred worries about children and whether the Beatles will ever regroup, cats and who engineered the assassination of Salvador Allende. Andy thinks about red beans, the Houston Astros and old Lefty Frizzell tunes.

This particular Sunday in September the six-thirty sun warmed their faces headed toward the Cypress tree. "I read in Rolling Stone that George sent letters to the others suggesting a final memorial tour; sort of a trip around the world." Mildred said. "That's annual," Andy answered, and nothing more was said of it that night.

The evening came on cooler than recently and Andy sat wrapped in a blanket, committed to leaving the furnace system shut down until November. Mildred never seemed bothered by extreme temperatures. She read an old collection of Cleanth Brooks essays. Andy was listening to a George Jones tape and reading *The Sporting News*.

"I'm afraid the Astros have fallen out of the pennant race," he said. "That's annual," Mildred answered and nothing more was said of it that night.

Bobby Bonds Remembering

The new sportswriter speculating trades
was a bat-boy for St. Vincent's B team
the year I broke in at Candlestick.
And the cheers, I mean cheers...

Listen, once against the Cubs, Tito told me,
from the right field seats several
City Lights clerks cheering
"Bah/bee   Bah/bee."
Wrists high, demanding a fast ball.

It's pride beats a hook thrower
He'll bend two or three and then
I see him heating up
and into that famous wind over again and over
"Bah/bee   Bah/bee."

The bat-boy sportswriter speculates a trade
for a banjo hitter and a left hander
I hit in my sleep.

Warming up

In his asphalt driveway George throws
against a cinder block wall a scuffed
green stained ball, his Larry Bowa model
increasingly consistent in reflex.

Carl puts his loose leaf binder,
a History of the Western Reserve
and a paper-bound Shakespeare down
on wet grass to join the game, less
practiced on defense, less patient.

Across the street, kicking through
piles of snow, Danny walks home.

Early in the Season

Outside under fiberglass awning
varsity players slide their bats
and catchers' gear into canvas bags
marked with the red Falcons logo.
The visiting bus drives away after
two innings and a long hour wait.
Inside a cage hung over hardwood floor
pings sound against pitches from a machine.
These bats do not crack and sophomores' socks
do not grip the glass smooth gym surface.
In the double doorway coach Moseley
clicks two pebbles in his left palm.

You Learned Photography
In Summer Term

I recognize exhaust fog which meets the air
where standard yellow busses warm up,
Kenny and Louise leaning against
the radiator grill, that pre-amateur
band off line formation on a scrap hard field.

Don't send me any too easy pictures
Bus colors do not change. Young musicians
will not improve and we are not
in that out of focus fieldhouse
waiting for the second half

After Halloween
We Let the Sun Go Down Early

Strict twigs clatter on gray-locked branches
chattering at two squirrels gone two weeks.
Across the brown stubble field picked clean
by the habits of sedentary animals
I see the only color left
in late light this November afternoon,
the blazed forehead of a rust red heifer.

After Spring Break

Jays dart among still bare branches and scold
starlings and sparrows away from feeders.
Robins, you can imagine, chuckle
and harvest crawlers from turf disturbed
by rain and students' shortcut footprints
across the landscaped campus lawn.

Somewhere it Might Be Spring

This gray and low volt morning shopkeepers
quietly trim yesterday's produce.
The neon lights still glow in windows
and broom men move along the street
pushing back the fall of last night's snow.
Slow dawn is winking out street lamps
at each untraveled intersection

Hardy's driver delivering lettuce
and potatoes stamped his too cold feet
outside the Manhattan Diner.
I work, he said, half a dozen
of these two cafe towns before lunch
and that many more each afternoon
for dinner spots and late night grills.

Ritual Occasions

Spring and summer Sunday afternoons
flower merchants parked their carts before
stone and wrought iron gates of cemeteries
where we went to visit the dead.
Young girls in bright taffeta dresses
and lace bonnets crossed cathedral grounds
with bought bouquets and their grandmothers
in somber kerchiefs carried garden sprays
to headstones with Czech and Hungarian
crosses beyond the newer graves.
We stood impatient behind and watched
the motionless hands of the tower clock.

In The Purchase Of Real Estate

Now make believe this fence built with pieces
of pine curves along your hill south
toward clumps of trees on the edge of town.
People lived here before the war
still want to cut across your lot short
to the post office or bakery.
You cannot devise sufficient
explanations for a two block circuit
to check their mail. Instead imagine
hinges swinging pine boards at the crest
of your hill and newcomers offering
Mince cookies or Bear Claws on their way home.

Blind Man's Bluff

I want no curtains on these windows
ground level and open to the street.
Everyone will watch me sitting
stare out past quarter crossed panes.
I want no curtains and no stained glass,
plain, clear glass in panes exposing
every move I do not make all day.

Make them turn their heads, avert their eyes
or look right through my bare windows
where Prospect Road bends west away
from my collapsing picket fence.
All of you will know I can see you
blush and turn aside on your way.

Nighttown Street Corner

Tomorrow I will tell at work, stories,
how the night mistreated me. Cloudbanks
stormed in late and carried little water
but stranded everything in place.
The sodden night divulged lights strung
down Front Street and cold damp controlled the town.
Refugees appeared hazed by the fog,
and the word I tried to read, stained by wet
from the newspaper ad on the sidewalk
near the gutter was bargains.

Thank You Note For A First Edition

I remember your simple stories,
the texture of their covers, impressions
of letter press platens in shades of red
title lines on off gray pages.
My fingers relax the limber collection
into my palm with tales of wet autumn
days and dust collecting on small town
dairy bars, the first neon light
in Garrett's window, your signatures stitched
onto tape bound for sewn spines.
People who know one another too well
trade conversations in intervals
you and I would like to share.

Now and Then
> "Every happy space is a child or grandchild of leaving."
> —Rainer Maria Rilke

Now when the cat has died in traffic
and performers moved to other glories,
already rooms empty on our second floor.
Away across the long backyard
you watch the ground skimmed with snow highlight
the brown fruit fallen from Buckeye trees,
our older neighbor stack cords of wood.
Across the square, the broad brick walked square,
you hear the bell ring in its stubby tower
and imagine students reluctant
on their way to Monday's first class.
Yet an immigrant in this orthodox country
you've learned the anticipated trails.
For once, that was then, you did
"walk into the breath not intended for you."

At Woodwinds and Reeds

Strange, the clerk thought you meant the weather.
No, you said, I mean instruments
like piccolos or penny whistles.
You know, blown in or blown over.
I laughed at his confusion
and you said, I need to practice.

I remembered your attractive practice,
your tunes running softly and your hands,
your long and limber fingers on
the instrument, the form of your lips
as you lift it toward your mouth.

In Some Heat and Hurry

We seemed not that young, not that long ago
and went on past every barrier.
No well meaning advice nor actual
obstacle stood in our way.
Your way was eager and hungry
and we kept on through bed slats
falling in the sweaty afternoon,
through everything, noon and night,
hot, cold, clean or a mess.
                              I miss that
and the clatter of bed slats
falling unheeded to the floor.

Off the Lakeshore

We named this once western land reserved
like friends holding your seats at folk concerts.
We forgot the Huron and Seneca
but they ask, if we are listening:

Have you walked these rolling hills and streams
and found the divide here where sticks
tossed into one might reach the Ohio
and into another drift back to the Lakes?

Who are you come lately to this place
with names and ways we can't understand?
Could you find your way back if we left
and you were staring at this wall of trees?
Do you have one story of the land
you heard from your fathers' grandfathers?

In The Office Numbered Con 4

Dusted webs hung in the corner
where we sat and beyond the wall
the orchestra rehearsed a modern fugue.
I sat by your window and you talked
of summer plans in Europe, perhaps,
if your fellowship came through.
Outside sunshine glistened on new leaves
still wet with early afternoon rain
and sprigs in the mud green grass.
You finger sheet music on your desk
and index cards on the standing file.
Plaster busts of pianists line your shelves.
Outside around two concrete ponds
workers trim branches showing no new growth..

Near Playhouse Square

Didn't you speak, call her name, maybe,
that Sunday outside the museum?

Yes, we sat on the bench facing the sun
the lean traffic moving toward the Lake.
I showed you that time capsule cover
Open in July, two thousand seventy-six.

Later that evening, inside from the rain
she played her guitar, Deep River Blues
and Trucker's Cafe and that song
that favorite song of yours.

On The Edge Of Town

On the front porch waiting for the breeze
to cool down this July evening
we listen to barely audible dogs
out on our road where asphalt gives way
to gravel and then to rutted dirt.
The dogs are familiar and Sunday
traffic slight this far out of town.

The breeze stays high in Walnut leaves
and sweat drops slide down my ribcage.
Our neighbor's inside lights appear
behind curtains hanging in open windows.
You bring out the last two longnecks
and we talk of Monday morning.

Office Hours

Like yesterday and the day before
rain dripping from second story eaves
sounds the same outside the window
and disturbs the same street puddles
with familiar irregular wrinkling.
I have seen this fog before distribute
light unevenly from florescent pods
atop the poles across the quad.
The same student voices chatter
past my open door and round the corner
this evening as the three before
and scribbles fingered in the misting pane
are all that have changed.

In This Barnyard

You are the rooster, man, in Poppa's barnyard
a bob slow bob head on your promenade
and you keep the hen-house always in view.
You are no ground bound rooster on two legs.
Your stubby wings lift you to the top rail
perch to sing out the screech of your song.
You have no time, rooster, for the bare yard
dance of scratch and peck for your own grain.
Keep singing your top rail song and keep
the henhouse always in your view.

An Explanation

You could have started elsewhere and walked
through that hailstorm of excuses
but, since you are here anyway,
figure it out.
                    I rubbed my forehead
above the separation of my eyebrows
and stared beyond the silence.

You could think of that slab headed cow's
long forehead with a nose buried
In the sere brown grass.
                        I saw the salt dome
Rising beyond the herd and some scrub pines
and said, you know no more than I.
He turned to look and shook his head.

Out of the Vapors of Rent and Habit
—Thomas McGrath

You may remember peculiar odors
of cheap duplicating machines
and duplicate black phones on back
to back desks in partitioned rooms.

You may still hear the steady tacking
of typists' keys and paper sliding
from tray to tray on those desks.

You knew standard recording procedures
retrieval devices and tedious
lines of named slots across four drawer files.

Stained crock china cups still litter
the southwest window sill where
drab green plants and one more technical
morning fade in the pale sun.

The Pretend Highwayman

Stand and deliver, he almost shouted.
Shout back, I thought, shout threats and noise.
Shout noise into these city streets.
He shouted again, Stand and deliver,
and I did deliver muttering all the while
veiled threats and promises of harm.
Stand and deliver, yourself, I muttered
but dug into near empty pockets
in my threadbare tan Dickies.
You are standing here, broad daylight,
claim a weapon in your jacket pocket
and can't hide a catch in your voice.

I had trouble believing the event
and still would, but for my empty wallet.
This is downtown Youngstown, you dip,
not some 1880s roadside.
Look, historian, hand over the goods,
and right now, or pay the price.
Pay, I said, this is all about pay.
We'll both pay the price and sooner
than any payday I can expect.

Here, take this Greenspan greenback,
my expired American Express card
and this queer twenty I was paid
for mucking filth out of some students'
college dorm rooms last July.

Take these membership cards in groups
I once joined and these photos of my wife
and kids gone ten months back to her mother's.
Take a dollar and seventy-three cents
and the front door key to a house
I once owned, and for god's sake
get a gun you aren't afraid to show.

An Eighth Grade Day

Clocks step away from their wall mounts
to march, precise infantry, through
crowded halls and Tuesday morning.
Their precision, the click of moments,
the clear chime of second period
move steadily beyond our reach.

Listen, students, a simple repetition
from the fixture we thought stationary.
You have my permission this morning
to do nothing, nothing at all.

Your assignment: sit on your home porch
or on your greening lawns if they're dry
in April sun. Watch the trees break out
into the air and do nothing else.
You are not required to report
your experience tomorrow.
Tomorrow you're not required to come in at all.

Junior English Substitute

Let me tell you something, all of you,
with your test papers marked too high
your letter jackets decorated
with championship patches
and all district medals pinned on.
Let me tell you something, all of you
who wear each others badges at the dance.

Look at this, all of these portraits
of Melville and Hawthorne, the Frost poem
on the bulletin board and listen
to each other's voices reciting
Lincoln's Address or Sojourner Truth's.

Discard your studied nonchalance
and look at the greening Cypress,
the sun working through morning haze.
and cafeteria staff coming to work.
Pay attention to things more wonderful
than your own semi-disguised worry.

Answering For A Mediocre Career

What have you done with all your potential, boy,
and where have you been? Where are your trophies,
the degrees you must have earned?
Mostly trading my days for dollars,
five years out there and ten back home.

They said you might make an engineer
or write the world's great story, boy.
I taught college students poetry
when we weren't just drinking beer.
I shook hands with politicians,
joined a farmers union fight.
Now I'm trying to make a habit
out of doing something right.

Better Things To Do

Day Labor

On South Main the torso shapes stand
in the front windows. Beside them stands
the laundress, dangles the clean shirt
around the torso shape, her hands
a moment on the shoulders, and mechanical
arms fold the sleeves. The laundress slips the shirt
away, packaged, and stacks it with others.
Each time the mechanical arms reach
she leans back, then forward and stacks
the packaged shirt. She sees the torso shape's
request and smiles, with her hands
a moment on the shoulders.

Inclusive Value

The old man with grey wire hair
started at the foot of his steps
walking steadily across his lot
until one arm's length separated us.
I have known your daddy
for forty-five years, boy.
On the derricks we worked twelve hour
shifts before he took us all
to your mother's dinner table.
You squander his name and stretch
my patience. Do not ride by here again
and give no one else such
clear excuse to hurt you.

April First

That green field deceives you, sucks
her hooves, heavy old cow on her way
to the grey barn. If I were a mare
this would cover my fetlock.
Listen to the brown cow walking.
You know the farmer did not choose
to leave his John Deere in this field.
Her burdened udder scrapes a furrow.
If I were fine lady, I would wince.

And The Weekly Conversation

The boy who lives in the house next door
walks out each Sunday morning with his large
wooden spoon and wraps cloth around the bowl end.
Each morning he walks across the street
to a green institutional dumpster
at the Inn kitchen door. The boy talks back
with his muffled spoon and dumpster metal side.
He talks back to the bell across the square.
Bang for tone, clank for boom the boy talks back
to the Sunday bell across the square.

Harvest

At the same time upstream men set ditches
and movable gates, older children
move across newly cleared ground planting
saplings in neat well-spaced rows.
Now each line of trees curves to bank
the flow of water those children
regulate at gates on intervals,
Monday, Thursday, Sunday, Wednesday.
Two miles downstream the men begin
to build the mill the children will use,
engines, pulleys, blades, chains and gears
to cut beams and boards from new growth
timber on plains too dry for crops.

Once A Dairy Farmer

Long after electricity
every night, every warm evening
he lights a lantern, a pale light.
The yard clear under a high bulb
casting no spell beyond its brightness,
he carries that pale light beyond
the yellow pool and past the hedge.

I see him walk away and sit
on his stone bench. Kerosene smells strong
on our porch and dogs bark in the dusk
at that pale flame in green lamp glass
carried out across the lighted yard.
He builds a mysterious country
beyond Live Oak and hanging moss, his lamp
and the strange cadence of bayou French.

Con Progression

Harriet in two years learned
the clarinet, to play it,
to miss no note, to keep silent
subtle time tensing the muscle
beneath her right knee her clarinet
perceptible on the beat.

Momma, I want to go after
that to Clarinet College.

In four years learned the college
entered the Philistine Philharmonic.

Momma, they needed another
woman for the E E O man.

I have an apartment across the street
from rehearsal hall, Momma. Now a step
wears into the curb by no other tread,
Momma, than mine.

Organizer

Knew this guy once 'n Juarez
Went by the name of Haysus LeeVase.
Spelled that L I V E S, claimed
Political ambition. Saw his name a lot,
bumper stickers, billboards, like that
Worked over Texas side, some pants factory
got involved in organizing, bilingual.
Had these cards, Ladies Garment Workers.
Management said he's some kind of fetish
pantyhose on the kitchen table
foundation garments in his bedroom.
Haysus kept at it though,
signed up the plant but got removed
on a morals charge.

Unemployed

I'm taking my two minute break
to relieve my ass infected
with one outrageous itch, my humongous
glove trapped in my left armpit freeing
my right hand to reach inside my belt
past the wrist for satisfaction
when our fresh faced foreman walks in.

"Darnel, you are neglecting your task."
I'm right back, "Your neglecting momma
Teach you that big old word."
"You'd best watch to whom you're speaking."
"If I could stand your face, I would."
"Darnel, I will have to write this up."

I pull my hand, whip the black marker
out of my right hip pocket
and hand it to the dude.

Working

I wish I worked for the railroad and rode
the Empire Builder east out of Seattle
each Tuesday in the afternoon. Board
I would say and stand dark blue aside
a clamor of crowds bound for Minneapolis.
Locomotive shafts would drive eight wheels
struggling out of King Street Station
as passengers settled into seats.

Straddling swaying aisles I'd determine
destinations for riders to St. Paul
sitting red tagged with those headed for
Spokane, Glacier, and Grand Forks,
and end my trips shifting comfortably
on a platform outside the diner
deadheading into Whitefish, Montana.

Singing The Expectation Blues

Early this autumn rock and plaster men
carefully oil their tools and talk much
of building office space and renovation.
Their trowels and knives, dusty mortar
palettes and tape put on racks
and hooks in hiring hall closets,
Sunday cribbage games, Thursday
family night bingo and a short winter.
Yes God, a short winter and a boom spring.

Better Things To Do

Sarah warped her back around the trunk
of a young pine tree where she sat
while sunshine flickered through the needles
onto her hands and knees and the dust
at her feet and softly she whistled
a tune learned early from her mother.

Her father called and called above the ricochet
of hoes chopping Into rocky ground.

Sarah watched two red tailed hawks slide
back and forth across the blue strip
she saw beyond the peaks of trees.
She listened to the ringing hoes move
away down the field, her father calling,
but Sarah's shoulders were stubborn,
her eyes full of two red tailed hawks.

Heading Home

I drove across back Ohio roads
through a town, believe this, Jelloway.
Houses in Jelloway crowd close
against the right of way at two curves.
Roadkill lay at the edge, no one
assigned to remove the carcass.
This November afternoon an Amish man
hauled hay through Jelloway.
Droppings from his two horse hitch
steamed like the breath of two men working
on an engine outside Bittner's Highway Service.

Retreat

My only boots need mending,
but I am no cobbler, a dealer
of camouflage clauses, the garbled
whispers passing October makes.
The patch on my roof loosens;
winter presses my carpentry.
I go backing past stations captured
short whiles ago as if here I might
stay this rout of every ambition.
I am no warrior, a dealer
of words and clauses.

Putting It Together
for Anne

My pants are part of some late
blooming project, flowers quilted
onto dark cloth faded blue along the legs,
the crotch seams split and left behind
last I took them off beside our bed.
I gave them to a warm legged woman
for quilting patch and patterned stitches.
Now all my careful lines beat time
to the rhythm of her machine
while leggings of my britches make patterns
with her stitches, warm legged woman
sewing patches in our house.

Other Work

What the River Gathers

I had in mind a river that begins
a surging brook in particular hills
and runs its course through meadows,
Pine and Cypress forests along the banks.
No drab abstraction, this river gathers
the surge of creeks and slower bayous,
ruptures dams and finally ignores them.

My river picks up pieces of the land
and brings trees and boulders with it.
People build well away from its flow,
even then on piers and pilings.
The river changes the look of the place
and the names of lesser rivers.
At last it gives its name to the bay.

Watching To Hear

Splash those sounds on your bare canvas.
Paint your way out of this roll of noise,
the whistle of steam in a kettle,
a wobbly wheel on the barrow unloading
bags of grain, the auctioneer's babble
after the cattle are sold.

Open your eyes and pay attention.
Start to listen, watch for some sound
to fall into place in your catalogue
of laughter, sermons and curses,
a hound's bay or nursery rhymes,
some tunes you don't quite remember.

Paying Attention

Ignore, for a moment, the traffic
at this intersection and concentrate
on the boy on the bench deserted
by public transportation systems
his feet dangling loose just above
the graffiti smeared sidewalk.
Duplicate his patience counting
each shoe swinging back and forth.
Disregard the changing stop light
and imagine the boy some evening
sitting against a Cypress tree
watching the red and white bobber
above his worm baited hook

Broken Obelisk
Houston, 1971

We lived there once before the moon men
or Brewster McCloud, before pool table felt
covered the playing space. End O'Main
was a dance hall on the south end of town.
We learned there once, before enlightenment
and liberal patrons, before we knew better.

Now it's changed, for the better, we're sure
and taller south end buildings block
The Midnight Special's twirling light.

My sister, though, still drinks Pearl
on summer evenings and that's a sign,
like the enlightened city council,
that we were well taught to mask our fear
of broken heads and broken monuments
and broken promises to those who lived there once.

Boom Times

Oil, boy, oil picked us up like a river
at flood stage and we surged along
the current of it, boy, rode the crest
of that river at high tide spitting
hands full of money with a common
disdain for your warnings, boy.

We rode that surge into town and out
again to derricks in new fields
until the flow slid back to eddys
stagnant in backwater pools, boy,
and we were factored out when
the bottom line was drawn above us.

Questionable Accuracy

I have seen, he said, saboteurs
gather after dark in alleys
or the walled gardens of patrons.
Men usually, now and again two women,
speak quietly of the great events
they will initiate tomorrow
among financiers and the armies
that enforce their restrictions.

I wonder why he tells these old stories,
where he may have heard them, and question,
out of reach of witnesses, their accuracy.

You can dig up your documents,
historian, and check for details.
You will not discover, in official records,
any names of betrayers nor mention
of valiant acts by defeated rebels.

In Answer to Your Letter with the International Reply Coupon Enclosed

You say it is spring there, Amberman
at the date oasis where you camp.
Mornings you build a fire of camel patties
and sometimes slabs of Palm bark.
Near your fire, you say, a pool glistens
below the well and two red roses bloom.
You say surely more are soon to come.

What keeps you, Amberman, there beneath
Palm trees near a glistening pool below the well?
Your friends ask what kept you there when all
the rest came home to better jobs.
The warmth of the fire, Amberman?
Or is it the rose, or roses to come,
that keeps you on that desert plateau?

Unexplanied Pilgrimage

I sat where Amberman said to sit,
watched him, stroke hobbled, angle up hill,
switch back and again in tall grass
through scattered Junipers toward the crest.
He sat some minutes out of sight
And returned much more slowly.

Walking back he did not explain himself
but stopped often to rub his left knee.
Near dusk, still half a mile from Bixby's,
he refused two ride offers.
Damp and cold slow the Amberman
but friends had waited in the warm tavern.

Tales Too Tall

This tale you've likely heard before,
disturbs your wandering inattention.
Listen to the nearly familiar details
of tales too tall for library shelves,
too vague for footnote references.

You have often ignored this voice
in the midst of nodding smiles that fail
regularly to mask your boredom.
Why now do these common place names
create such unexpected interest?

You have been most of these places
and heard many of these stories
you know are imagined.
On this Tuesday, though, even Billings
sounds like fun and the river stories
this time might be true.

An Amberman Afternoon

Another time after nothing happened
you flipped your hammer one full turn
into the air before the handle
slapped back into your right palm.
Marking time with your simple flips
you kept the claw up without looking.

A Thursday ritual digression
if I walked over from the office
with work slow and the shop empty.
You told more of those messages
I did not want to hear, checks against
my too easy notions of progress.

Minimum Wage

Employees of a privately held
corporation, sharing our drowsy
monologues after another close
and brutal day, we speak our discontent
in mostly confidential outrage.

All the reports filed properly
away, only a few incomplete
spaces left intentionally empty
to protest the careful payroll ledgers
kept spare by regular layoffs.

Red Dirt Summer

On the bank that set backwater off
from Black Duck Bay we found a leaky boat
and Scott christened it Agate Ill.
One Saturday late in June, missing
the double feature we launched her
from live oak trees and hanging Spanish moss
and polled across stagnant water,
thigh deep when we were forced
to pull her across to the farther bank.

In hot sun on the asphalt lot
at Pay-and-Pak we sat until nearly dry
and walked to The Palace in town
and then back home for cover.
Gary told anyway and pointed
to scum stains on our jeans and tee shirts.

Red Dirt Summer II

Scott's finger traced a circle in red dirt
where we spread our marbles. He shot first,
hollered 'Keeps" but I heard no question
and hunkered to the game after his miss.
Afternoon sweat streaks collected dust
on our arms and bare backs bent over
that circle trimmed with knuckle prints.

Called to supper we threw two marbles
at his little brother playing in a sandbox
shaded by two Chinaberry trees
near the corner of the garage.
We ran laughing to eat on the porch,
laughing because it was July.

Waiting for Breakfast

Like the spinning yo-yo of a child
your dreams no longer come back awake.
They catch on their string, a sprung momentum
twirling askew the line in your hand.
You rearrange your twisting dreams
to the spool of your new intention.

You may wake up tomorrow picturing
all you did Thursday, years ago.

I know the man in the saddle
as the backhoe bucks and tears chunks
away from the earth on one empty lot
left among unfinished building shells
and freshly poured concrete slabs.
I know the children who played here
Thursday, thirty-seven years ago.

Tracking The Time

Beneath willows greening early
Darnell sees Sonja and Wilson talking
with gestures and waving arms, turning
their bodies to punctuate changes
in stories the sisters tell one another.
Darnell has worked in their father's
store since Sonja was born.
Wilson took her first steps that year
while Darnell sat the girls and the store.
Next week Sonja will join her sister
when she returns for summer term
to her well regarded high school.

Lyrics Never A Song

A lonely cold corner in an empty cafe
with no one around to hear you play,
you drummed out your rhythms and wrote down
your words to at least fifteen songs everyday.

The owners don't like you, the servers don't care,
your stomach as empty as booths you can see
and the fry cook's just waiting to close.
The traffic on seventh passes by in your sight
and outside's as deserted as in.

I took a long time to get here flat broke
and sure won't go back where I've been.
I spent two years in Memphis and two in Hot Springs
and I've been here in Texas since May.
It makes little difference where my letter's postmarked
if I write fifteen songs everyday.

Imagining One More Conversation

Remember, Emiliano, two boulders
where we sat around our fire
in October not two hundred yards
beyond your back fence, camping out
and cooking meat patties in tin foil
your mother made in her kitchen?

We had a creek though, Emiliano,
a gurgle of water dripping over
stones and pebbles toward the culvert
under Garth Road. We had a creek
and Live Oak trees hung with Spanish moss,
Blackberry brambles and those boulders.

Were we ever out there past nine?
That year you got your nickname
because you stood three inches shorter
than Emil Torsen and Mister Pietsch said

Oh, well, you'll remember all that.
Even that year, we were fourteen
and came in to sleep in your bedroom.

I bought those bunk beds, Emiliano
from your mother when she moved
and used them side by side for years
in our two girls' corner bedroom.

In The Stuffed Envelope

My older brother had a picture of this girl. He had been in first and second grades with her in Pittsburgh and she gave him her picture when he was moving away. Glenda, he said this girl's name was Glenda and he kept the picture ever since. It's still here in the stuffed envelope they sent me, the stuff from his apartment.

When I was about ten he said I could not have Glenda's picture. One year I offered him three baseball cards for that picture. He said no - even to Lou Boudreau. I didn't know Glenda, but I worried about her head. In that picture her head seemed so large, and I worried her body would never grow to match her head.

I didn't know Glenda and he never told me her last name. Now, I have her picture and wish I could write her. I'd like to ask her if she remembered my brother from second grade.

Men of the Church

Our fathers were steady ushers, Charlie.
Sunday after Sunday morning they stood
aside the double doors, greeted friend
and neighbor with illustrated worship guides.
By word and gesture our fathers sent them
to their familiar weekly places
and led others to appropriate pews.
But our fathers grasped the late elbows
of younger widows, Charlie, and gently
led them toward more discrete seating.

The Night Rider

Evenings you must ride the same near empty bus
to town and watch, at stops across the street,
as crowds depart and walk toward home.
At half past five you transfer and ride,
standing, with my homebound crowd
until seats come empty two stops from mine.

Where are you going, I wonder,
and what will you do when you arrive?
McLean runs three shifts at his sawmill
a quarter mile past route's end
and a few shops are open nights.
Maybe, though, you have night classes,
an older student at the college.

South Broadway Bus

She tried, patiently, and again to fit
the brown cloth glove over the stiff fingers
of his right hand held out like a spined disk.
Bumps and our driver's inconsistent speed
added to his tremored agitation.
Frustrated, he dropped his arm
"It's not that cold anyway."

At thirty-second street the route
turned south for residential stops
and we were well short of half full
at Broadway as she waited for his
brown gloved hands to grasp the walker
she held outside the kneeling door
and the few of us left looked away.

That Was Years Ago

Picking through the rubbish of an uneventful day
you will count each coin and smooth wrinkled bills
along the edge of your bedside table.
Now carefully record each receipt
or from memory the minor expenses
and drop used foil wrappers one by one
into your nearby waste basket.
My fingers are clumsy with your unmatched buttons.
I know your underwear is not lace
the uneven filigree of scrub board and wringer washers.
The stockings on your floor are not sheer.

After that I notice trinkets chipped
and glued together on pasteboard boxes
you use for a chest of drawers.
On your kitchen floor turf carpet
salvaged from the funeral parlor next door,
the only shoes you ever wear thrown loose
I wonder if you went outside barefoot.
You returned from the washroom you share
with three neighboring apartments,
surprised I'm still sitting at your table.

A Small Orchestra

Dulcimers, strummed and hammered softly
by mountain quartets playing your song,
and crowds clamored and clapped to hear them.
Their bone picks and soft hammers sound loud
enough in the backyards where you played.
with visiting guitars, sometimes a mandolin.

Now your small orchestra plays weekends
at Barton's and neon signs spell out your name.
I waited last Sunday in the rain
under the awning at the campus bar
and they told me you called Tuesday
during my Church History lecture.

Going To and Fro Upon the Earth

One morning late in October
she turned south across the bridge over the river
and walked up the path to the boulder
where the trail turns steep to the west
along the ridge back to the highway.

Against a crumbling wall where old men pee at night
we found seven sketches we had not seen.
The lines ran away from loose centers
unable to hold themselves together.

No one knew what brought her to this alley
behind a line of Front Street saloons
or why she left her seven sketches here.
But she knew the questions we would ask
and the wondering stares she would leave behind.

Autumn Walk

Mornings when the air is crisp and
muted colors show bright in the sun
we walk the Gabriel's bank, its flow
limited by October's lengthy drought.
You exclaim the rust colored Cypress
the brown and white limbs of Sycamores
and dust green leaves on Post Oaks.
You call attention to two Great Egrets
flying late from their upstream roost,
the reflecting glisten of the river
flowing slowly over low stones.

The Great Blue Heron

You ran late after Sunday's ringing bells.
and bright sun pushed tree shadows along
your road toward the low water bridge.
In a backwater off the river
you watched a heron as if on one leg
consider the stream and Cypress forest
beyond the shallow reed marshes.
An aviary of smaller birds
flittered along the mud banks and low limbs.
On a long neck the heron turned her head
spread her unexpected wings and
lifted silently toward sunlight.

What We Left Behind

When the earth cries out Human
who is left to answer?
When the people call out Friend
will they hear an audible response?
Where are the friends who walked among
Pine and Pin Oak trees on red hills
and knew the names of things?

When the earth cries out Human
we are not there to answer.
Our plows did not cut these furrows
and we will not harvest their crops.
We have found new places to grow old
places we did not work with our hands
where no people we've ever known have died.

A Half-Sonnet for Anne

Now you strum four shorter strings
your reach spans fewer keys.
And now you choose the quieter songs
and sing some lower tones,
yet music is your native tongue
your language and your joy.
And still your voice rings clear a chime
that fills my heart and ear.

Losing My Way

I am living off the dust of red dirt
stirred into acorn meal and hand shakes
meaning less than nodding heads,
wandering back and forth across country
where you have blazed few guidelines.
You may not hear, as you should, my desire
ringing against one more drab morning.

Scatter your grace across my trail.
Flag the right of way with benedictions
hung high in Spanish moss on Cypress.
Seal off these endless false trails and call out
my route across this swamp silent maze.
Bridge my chord and play all my notes with your
long fretting fingers and soft running tune

An Afterword

On a back shelf in our garage
when we were planning to move I found
a dusty box of notebooks we must
have moved three or four times before.
This time, in a chair we've left behind,
I sat and read from pages dated
nineteen seventy eight and eighty,
notes on reading Rilke and Hart Crane.

We have that box with us now, the notebooks
no longer edge dusted and the pages
reread for lines of verse to compare
with pages on these newer bookshelves.
You may hear from page to page
the sound of a different voice,
perhaps a mellowed yearning.

    I thank Stephan F. Austin State University Press and the Director, Kimberly Verhines for their continued commitment to publishing poetry and for her help and hard work on this collection. Many folks, some knowingly, have encouraged me and helped much in this gathering. I want especially to thank Dana Hendrix and O.L. Davis, Bruce Glasrud, Jenni Jordan, Dan K. Utley, and Kyle Wilkison.
    I thank Anne. Without her few of these poems would have filled my life or entered my mind.

www.ingramcontent.com/pod-product-compliance
Lightning Source LLC
Chambersburg PA
CBHW060532080526
44586CB00012B/712